PLANET EARTH
AND THE UNIVERSE

Planet Guides

Planet Earth
and the Universe

Duncan Brewer

MARSHALL CAVENDISH
NEW YORK · LONDON · TORONTO · SYDNEY

Reference Edition Published 1993

© Marshall Cavendish Corporation 1992

Published by Marshall Cavendish Corporation
2415 Jerusalem Avenue
PO Box 587
North Bellmore
NEw York 11710

Series created by Graham Beehag Book Design

Library of Congress Cataloging-in-Publication Data

Brewer, Duncan, 1938-
 Planet earth / Duncan Brewer,
  p. cm. - (Planet guides.)
 Includes index.
 Summary: Examines the physical characteristics and conditions of the Earth, describing its position in relation to the sun and other planets and surveying humanity's attempts to penitrate its mysteries.
  ISBN 1-85435-368-3 (set). - ISBN 1-85435-371-3
 1. Earth - Juvenile literature. [1. Earth.] I. Title.
 II. Series: Brewer, Duncan, 1938- Planet guides.
 QB631.4.B74   90-40809
                                                       CIP
                                                        AC

Printed in Malaysia by Times Offset Pte Ltd

SAFETY NOTE

Never look directly at the Sun, either with the naked eye or with binoculars or a telescope. To do so can result in permanent blindness.

Acknowledgement

Most of the photographs, maps and diagrams in this book have been kindly supplied by NASA.

Title Page Picture:
This outstanding photograph of the sphere of the Earth was taken from the Apollo 17 spacecraft during the final lunar landing mission.

Contents

Introduction

There is nothing like intergalactic space for cutting the human race down to size. Space probes push out beyond the *planets*. Ever more powerful telescopes and imaging equipment back on Earth have brought the far

Edwin "Buzz" Aldrin was the second man to set foot on the Moon. Neil Armstrong, who took this photograph, was the first man on the Moon; he can be seen reflected in Aldrin's helmet visor.

reaches of the *Solar System* into focus and opened up previously unknown regions of the universe beyond our own *galaxy.*

Tiny Earth

A person stumbling on an ants' nest may laugh to see the tiny creatures rushing around, self-importantly performing their minute tasks. Yet men and women must now come to terms with the fact that they live on one of the smaller planets *orbiting* a rather ordinary *star* – the Sun – toward the edge of a commonplace galaxy containing thousands of millions of such stars. And this galaxy, the Milky Way Galaxy, is just one of thousands of millions of other galaxies in the universe.

The Solar System occupies a tiny corner of the Milky Way Galaxy. From Earth, we see the Milky Way as a pale band of millions of stars. The Sun, which dwarfs all other bodies in the Solar System, is just another Milky Way star.

7

The Big Bang

Physicists believe that about 15,000,000,000 years ago, there was a vast explosion in the emptiness of space. This explosion, usually referred to as the Big Bang, marked the moment of birth of the universe of which we are a part.

The First Few Seconds

Before the Big Bang, there was nothing that we would recognize as physical material, not even *atoms*. In the first ten-thousandth of a second of this explosion, unimaginably high temperature and density helped to create some of the first building blocks from which atoms are formed. These pieces of matter are known today as quarks and mesons.

As the Big Bang hurled this primitive material outward in all directions, the temperature and the density began to fall. The building blocks began to stick together to form the sub-atomic particles – protons and neutrons that are at the core of atoms. Only ten seconds had passed. The primal material continued to fly outward on the wings of the explosion.

Star Birth

In the first few minutes after the Big Bang, with temperatures of at least 18,000,000°F (10,000,000°C), nuclear reactions started to create the basic structures of the gases hydrogen and helium. Over the next million years, the radiated energy of light and heat stemmed from the

Did You Know?

The word *galaxy* comes from the Greek for milk, "gala." Ancient Greeks believed the Milky Way was formed from milk spilled from the breast of the goddess Hera while she fed Heracles (Hercules).

original explosion. The long process of the formation of the first stars began.

At first, the new atoms joined up into a thin cloud of hot gas. The radiation that kept the atoms moving eventually weakened as millions of years passed. Atoms began to cluster together. Eventually, what had been an evenly distributed gas cloud became a large number of huge, separate clumps of gas. The force of *gravity* is exerted by all objects in the universe. It played a major part, first in the grouping of the gas globules that would become clusters of galaxies, and eventually in the formation of the stars within the galaxies.

Last Traces

Most of that enormous initial heat has disappeared. A relic of it still persists and is measurable as a faint, background microwave radiation, now only a few degrees above the lowest possible temperature of *absolute zero*. The most obvious proof of the Big Bang theory is the fact that everything in the universe is moving away from everything else.

Think of a blueberry muffin with blueberries fairly evenly distributed all the way through it. Now think of that muffin growing steadily larger and larger, as if it were being inflated with a pump. As the muffin expands, the blueberries grow farther apart from one another, although they stay in the same positions relative to one another. In the expanding universe, the blueberries are the galaxies.

Did You Know?

Our galaxy is so huge that a flash of light traveling at its natural speed of 670,000,000 miles (1,080,000,000 km) per hour would take 100,000 years to travel from one side of the galaxy to the other.

Building Blocks

When you look up at the night sky with the naked eye, everything you see is part of the Milky Way Galaxy, our own star system The stars and gas clouds of our galaxy obscure our view of other galaxies, although we can see some of them with the aid of powerful telescopes.

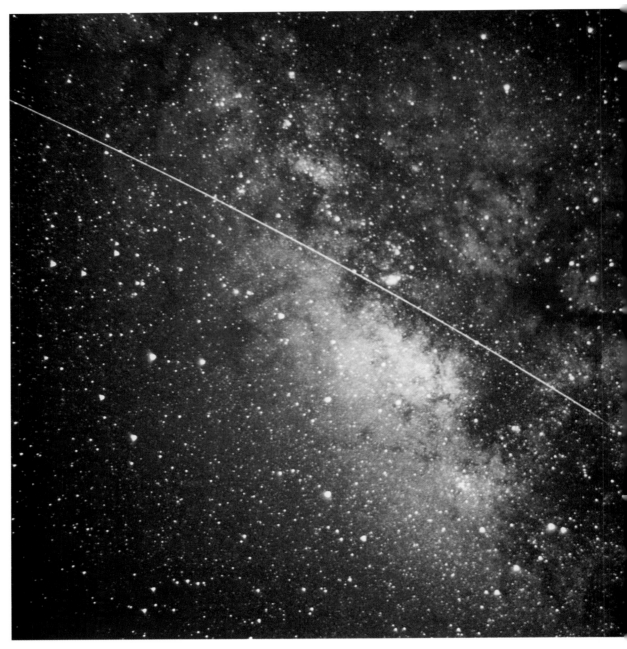

The galaxies are spread very thinly through the emptiness of space. They are swirling, dynamic systems in which matter comes together to form stars, *planets, satellites, asteroids* and *comets*. The speed at which other galaxies move away from us – due to the expansion of the "blueberry muffin" universe – is known as their *radial velocity*. Those farthest away from us move faster than those close to us.

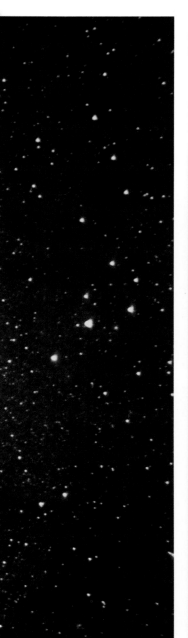

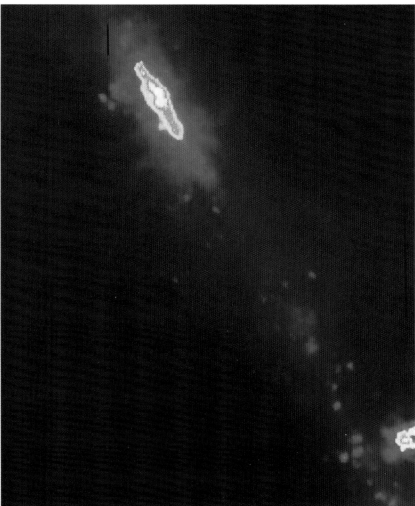

Expanding Universe

Astronomers have worked out a way of calculating the radial velocity of other galaxies. They can do this because of a phenomenon known as the *Doppler effect*. Have you ever heard an express train blow its whistle as it rushes past you? The sound starts off high-pitched, and then slides down the scale to a lower

Emitting a far higher level of infrared radiation than our Milky Way Galaxy, this galaxy was photographed using the 7·2-foot (2·2-meter) telescope at Mauna Kea, Hawaii.

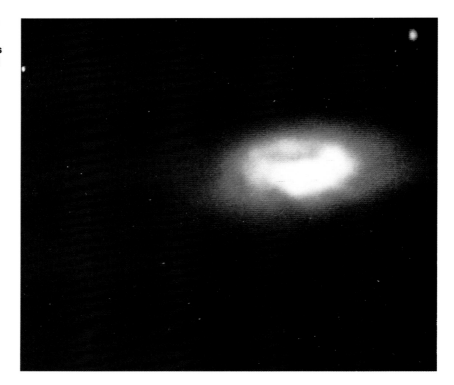

The Trifid Nebula is formed from great clouds of hydrogen and dust, bright with the glow of new, hot stars.

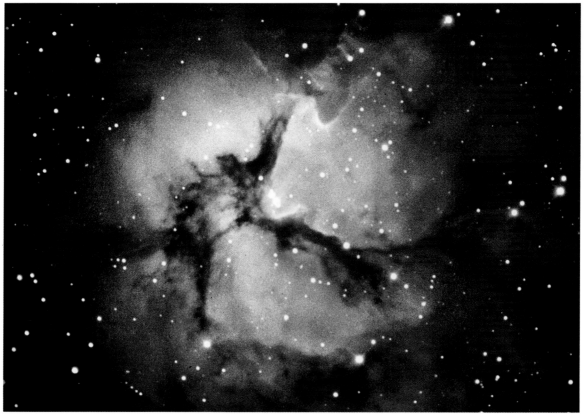

pitch as the train passes. This change is the result of the Doppler effect. If you know what the whistle's true pitch is, it is possible to calculate the train's speed from the change of pitch.

Similarly, when a galaxy moves away from the viewer, its light takes on a redder "pitch." This is known as the *red shift.* Those galaxies farthest from us appear the

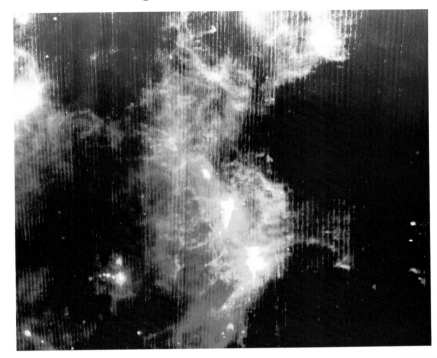

This IRAS image of the Constellation Orion and its surroundings shows different infrared intensities as different colors.

The Ring Nebula galaxy in Lyra is a great spherical shell of glowing gas, with a small, hot, white dwarf star at its core. The gaseous shell is half a light year across.

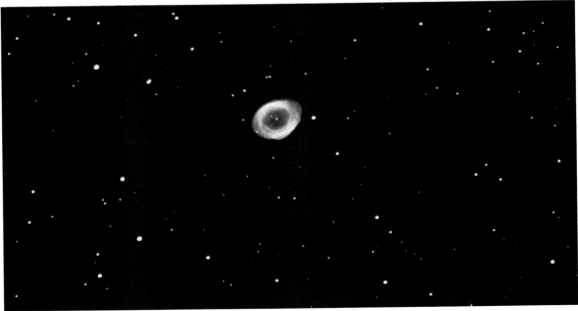

reddest, showing that they are moving the fastest, and confirming that the universe is constantly expanding.

Galaxies come in different shapes and forms, most of them spiral. Like the Milky Way, most of the galaxies contain thousands of millions of stars. They usually have a concentration of stars toward the center, forming a bright "nucleus." Spiral galaxies have great trailing, spiral "arms" radiating from the center; the spiral arms are made up of millions of stars. Our Sun is such a star, situated in a spiral arm toward the outer edge of the Milky Way Galaxy.

A negative photo of the Constellation Orion, showing the main stars. Orion is well known to naked-eye observers. The Sword of Orion hangs down from the three stars of Orion's belt and contains the red glow of the Great Nebula in orion, or Orion Molecular Cloud.

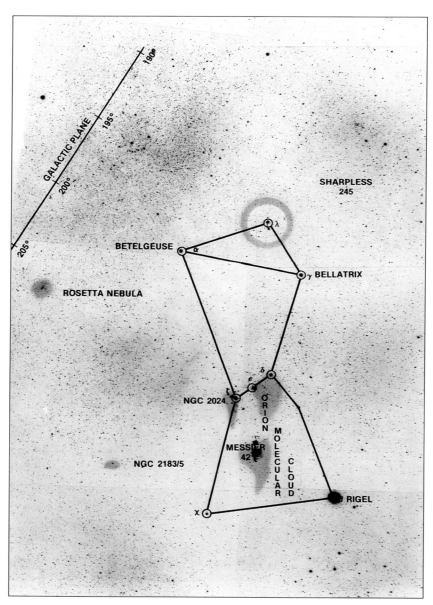

Time Travel

Astronomers often measure distances through space in terms of the speed of light. A *light year* is the distance covered by a beam of light in one year. It takes light from our Moon one-and-a-quarter seconds to reach us. Therefore, the Moon is one and a quarter light seconds away from us. Many of the objects we see through telescopes are many light years away. If a star is 100 light years away, we are in fact seeing it as it appeared 100 years ago.

Spiral galaxies look like whirling lawn sprinklers spraying water. The arms, which lie in a flat plane, curve outward from the central bulbous hub of concentrated stars.

One light-year is the equivalent of 5,878,000,000 miles (9,460,000,000 kilometers). Another measurement used by astronomers is the *"parsec,"* which is equivalent to about 3·26 light years.

The great disk of the Milky Way is 100,000 light years across and rotates slowly around its center. The stars nearer the center rotate faster than those farther out. Our own Sun completes a circuit of the galaxy about once every 250,000,000 years.

Beyond the Milky Way Galaxy

Another galaxy relatively close to the Milky Way Galaxy is the Great Galaxy in Andromeda. It has a similar flattened, rotating form, with a concentration of stars forming a central nucleus, and a globular halo of stars surrounding the flattened disk. The Grat Galaxy Andromeda is 2,250,000 million light-years away.

Some galaxies are so far away, and so faint, that it is difficult even for experts to make them out on the images on photographic plates taken using large telescopes. Astronomers have recently developed a technique for scanning the plates with lasers and then using superfast computers to enhance very faint features. In this way, astronomers have started to discover a large number of new galaxies.

In this image of the Great Galaxy Andromeda, the outer spiral arms can be seen separated from the central nucleus by dark bands of galactic dust.

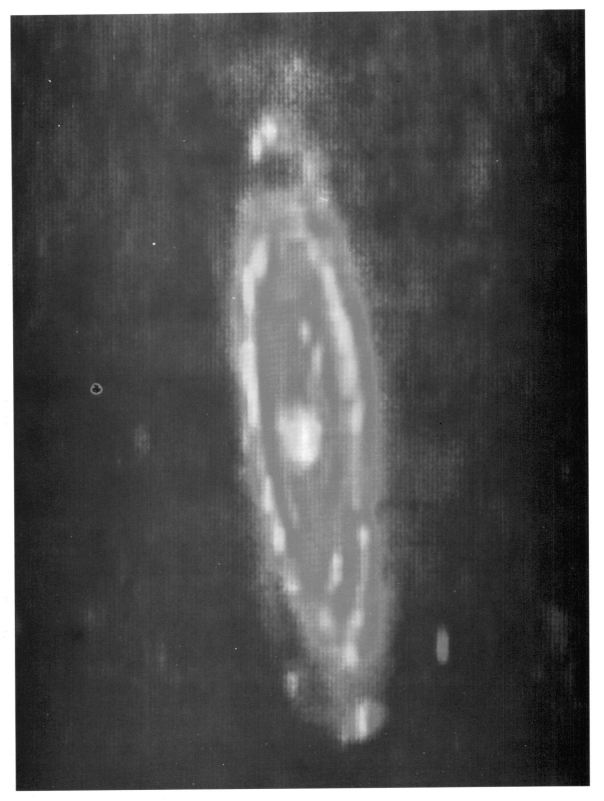

The Solar System

The stars have patterns to their lives. They are born, live, grow old, and finally die. Some go through this cycle of life and death far faster than others. The more massive they are, the brighter they shine, and the faster they pass through the stages of their development.

Our Sun is an average sort of star, middle-aged and medium-sized. It started to shine about 5,000,000,000 years ago. It should continue to do so for another 5,000,000,000 years before it has exhausted its supply of hydrogen fuel.

A Star is Born

Like other stars, our Sun began life as a large *mass* of gas contracting under its own gravity. A bicycle pump becomes hot at the end as you pump. This happens because, when gases are under pressure, they increase in temperature. When a star is born, a gas cloud contracts. The temperature rises in its center, and, at about 18,000,000°C, a change begins to take place in hydrogen, transforming it into helium. This is called the "hydrogen burning" phase of the star, when it begins to shine. It is this that produces light.

Eventually, as the hydrogen becomes exhausted, the helium core starts to contract again. At the same time, the star's outer layers expand, and the star grows into what is known as a "red giant." When stars can contract no further, some become "white dwarves," with a

Did You Know?
Because we live inside the Milky Way Galaxy, it is difficult to see its shape. Astronomers have worked out that it is shaped like a giant spiral about 100,000 light years in diameter.

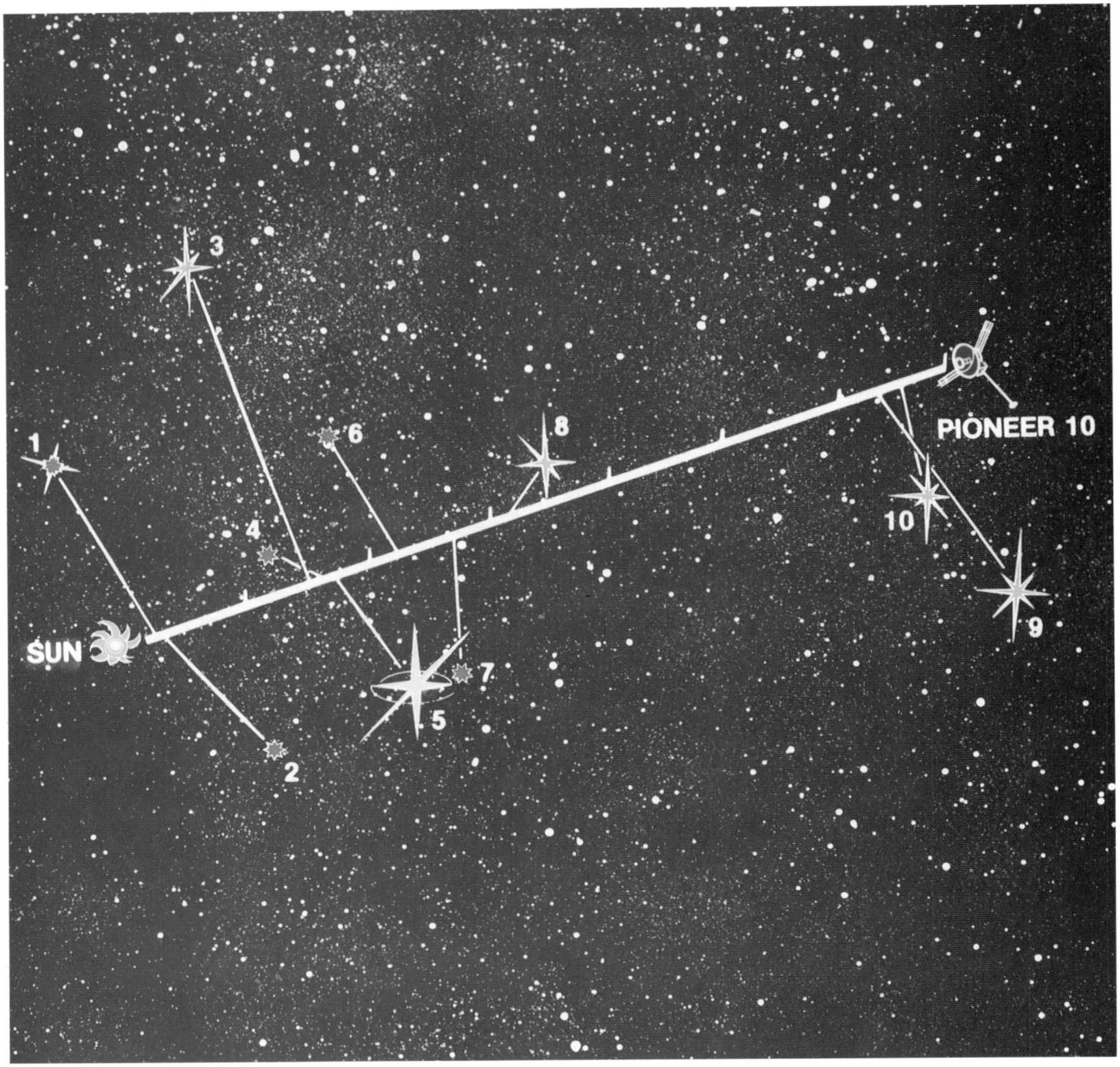

Moving outward across the galaxy, Pioneer 10 will pass relatively close to different types of stars, including red dwarves, like Proxima Centauri, and solar-type stars similar to our Sun. Proxima Centauri is No. 1 on the diagram. It will take the probe more than 26,000 years to come within 6·38 light years of it.

close-packed core of either helium (in stars less than 0·4 times the mass of the Sun) or carbon and oxygen (in stars between 0·4 and 8 times the mass of the Sun).

Supernova Factories

The most massive stars develop a core of iron. When the temperature has built up to billions of degrees, the center collapses. There is a massive "*supernova*" explosion that flings the star's substance out into space.

The birth and death of stars is the process that creates the chemical elements that make up everything in our world – including us. Stars operate like factories, creating these elements in the furnaces of their own contractions.

A supernova explosion can have the brightness of a million suns. It can also produce elements like uranium. All of these star-born elements ultimately end up floating in space as parts of gas clouds. They will, in turn, be the beginnings of future stars, and maybe planets as well. The Big Bang produced hydrogen and helium. All other elements were created in the first few billion years of the universe by supernova explosions.

This supernova remnant survivor of a supernova explosion in the seventeenth century, is situated in the constellation of Cassiopeia. We can "see" its remains only by X-rays and radio-waves. The exploding star that created them was almost 100 times as large as the Sun.

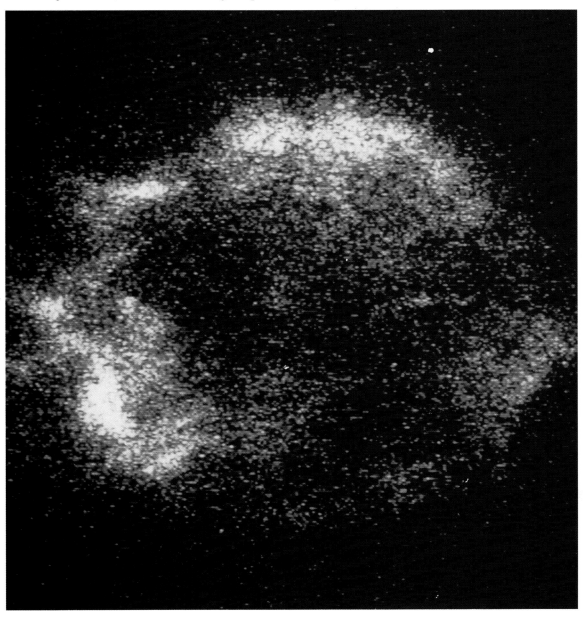

The Vela supernova remnant, seen in this X-ray image, has a pulsar at its center. It emits pulses of radio activity once every 0·089 seconds.

Kingdom of the Sun

The Solar System consists of the Sun and those bodies, such as planets, satellites, asteroids, and comets, which are trapped by the Sun's gravity into a variety of orbits around it. The Milky Way Galaxy had been in existence for billions of years when the Sun was born. Millions of stars had been born and died. In the gaseous swirls of the galaxy, they left an ever-richer "soup" of chemical elements locked in gases and dust. They provided the raw materials for future stars and planets. A cloud of gas and dust began to congeal, possibly triggered by the

Vega, the third brightest star in our night sky, is 26 light-years from Earth. It may be at the center of a younger Solar System in the making. Only a fifth the age of our Sun, it is surrounded by solid particles up to the size of asteroids, which could in time combine to form planets.

birth or explosive death of a nearby star. As it spun, it became denser and heated up until it reached ignition point. The Sun was born.

Birth of the Planets

The new Sun did not use up all of the available material in the rolling gas cloud from which it was formed. While the Sun began to shine with fusion reactions, particles in the cloud around it began to congeal to form other,

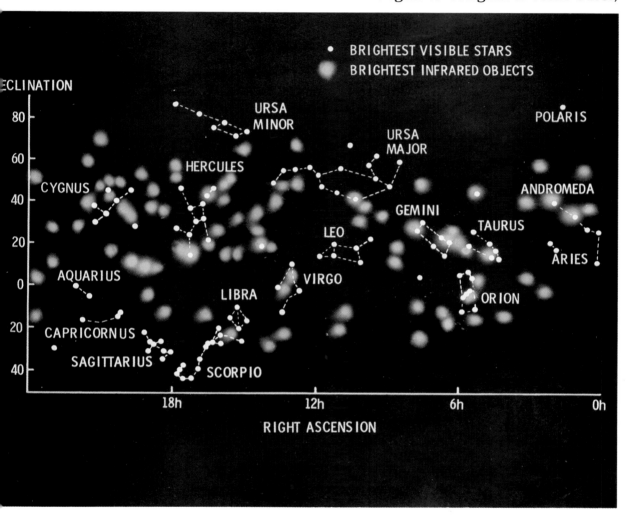

Infrared imaging enables us to see far more stars than are visible to the naked eye and optical telescopes. The stars we see optically are warm enough to radiate visible light. Many more are too cool to appear unless we use infrared imaging techniques.

23

much smaller, bodies. These were the planets. Scientists differ in their theories concerning the origins of planetary material. Some think the planets originated in the same gas and dust clouds from which the Sun condensed. Others believe the Sun's gravitational pull may have attracted material from *interstellar space.*

Almost certainly, as the Sun was formed, it was surrounded by a flattened, rotating disk made up of many clumps of material. A long series of collisions helped to coalesce some of these clumps into sizeable bodies. As time passed, they, in turn, "mopped up" any smaller fragments that came within range of their fields of gravity. Some heated up enough to melt as they contracted. The heavier materials then became concentrated in the central core.

Orbital Wanderers

The nine planets, of which the Earth is one, orbit the Sun at different speeds. If we view them from the Earth's northern hemisphere, they move in a counterclockwise direction. The planets also spin, or rotate, at different speeds in a counterclockwise direction – except for Venus and Uranus, which both have a retrograde rotation, that is they spin in the other direction.

The orbits of the planets are elliptical, like ovals or flattened circles. The closest point of an elliptical orbit to the Sun is called the *perihelion,* and the point farthest away is the *aphelion.*

Compared to the Sun, the planets are tiny. All together, they have only one-thousandth of the mass of their parent star. The distance between the planets and the Sun is often given in *astronomical units.* One astronomical unit is the average distance of the Earth from the Sun, about 93,000,000 miles (150,000,000 kilometers). Mercury, the nearest planet to the Sun, orbits it at an average distance of 0·387 AU. The average distances of the other planets from the Sun are as follows: Venus 0.723 AU; Earth 1.0 AU; Mars 1.524 AU; Jupiter 5.203 AU; Saturn 9.539 AU; Uranus 19.18 AU; Neptune 30.06 AU; Pluto 39.44 AU.

The orbits of most of the planets are very close to the plane of the Earth's orbit, varying from it from as little as 0°46' (Uranus) up to 3°24' (Venus). The two exceptions are Mercury, which has an orbital inclination of 7°, and Pluto, which has an orbital inclination of 17°12'.

Below: When we illustrate the relative sizes of the planets, we can see that Earth is tiny beside the gas giant like Jupiter and Saturn. They, in turn, are dwarfed by the Sun.

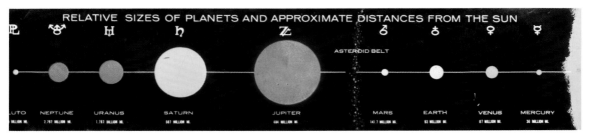

RELATIVE SIZES OF PLANETS AND APPROXIMATE DISTANCES FROM THE SUN

ASTEROID BELT

PLUTO	NEPTUNE	URANUS	SATURN	JUPITER	MARS	EARTH	VENUS	MERCURY
	2,797 MILLION MI.	1,787 MILLION MI.	887 MILLION MI.	484 MILLION MI.	141.7 MILLION MI.	93 MILLION MI.	67 MILLION MI.	36 MILLION MI.

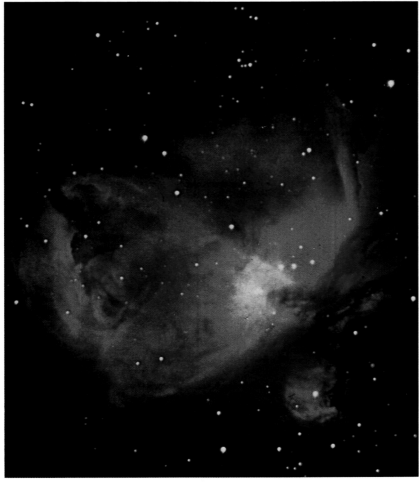

Left: Planets can appear to be so small in the sky that it is almost impossible to spot them. However, some night-sky features, such as the distinctively ruddy Great Nebular in Orion, can be found without the aid of a telescope.

25

Planetary Years and Days

The closer they are to the Sun, the faster the planets orbit it. This is due to a sort of planetary survival technique. The closer to the Sun, the stronger is the pull of its gravity. Objects near the Sun have to move faster to avoid being pulled right into the Sun itself. Mercury orbits the Sun once every 88 days. Pluto, which is, for most of its orbit, the most distant planet known to us, takes 247·7 years to travel just once around the Sun. The orbital period is the planet's year. Thus, Earth's orbital period is 365·26 days, one complete Earth year.

Another major difference in the performance of planets is the time each takes to rotate upon its own axis. Speeds vary from a few hours to a few months. The fastest is Jupiter, rotating on its axis once every 9 hours 50 minutes. The slowest is Venus, rotating once every 243 days. Earth rotates once every 23 hours 56 minutes. Each rotation measures a new day.

The Earth is located toward the edge of the Milky Way Galaxy, which is 100,000 light years across, and from its center, an observer would see the Earth as it was about 30,000 years ago.

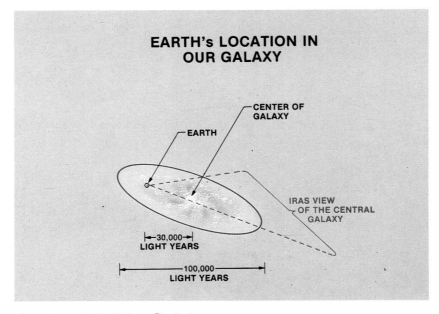

EARTH's LOCATION IN OUR GALAXY

CENTER OF GALAXY

EARTH

IRAS VIEW OF THE CENTRAL GALAXY

30,000 LIGHT YEARS

100,000 LIGHT YEARS

Orbits Within Orbits

Just as the planets rotate around the Sun, the moons or satellites of the Solar System rotate around their parent planets. Earth has only one moon, and both Mercury and Venus are moonless. Mars has two moons, while Jupiter, Saturn and Uranus have 16, 18, and 15 respectively. Pluto, like Earth, has just one moon. Neptune has eight, including six tiny satellites discovered by the Voyager space probe in 1989.

Viewed edge-on by the IRAS telescope, the Milky Way Galaxy reveals knots of interstellar gas along its length.

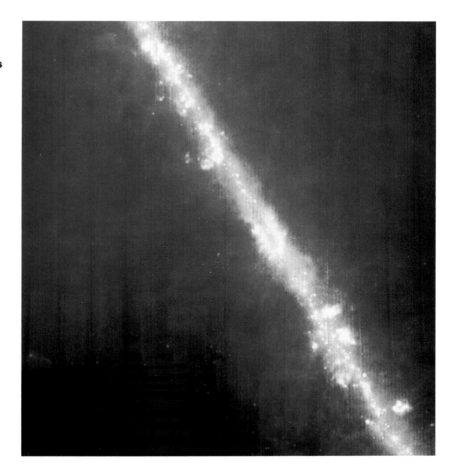

Ultraviolet photography reveals the Earth's broad halo of low-density hydrogen, known as the geocorona, as seen from Apollo 16, the next-to-the-last Moon lander in the Apollo series.

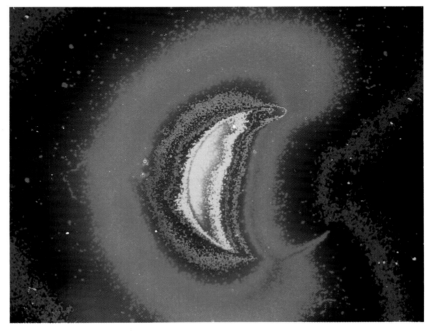

Astronomy and the Planets

All planets are dark; the light that appears to shine from them is the reflected light of the Sun. The stars, on the other hand, shine with the luminosity of their own burning energy. When early star-gazers began to look closely at the night sky, they traced the patterns of the stars in their fixed *constellations* and noted the apparent movement of the constellations across the sky. But they could see little or no difference between the stars and the planets. They were all just points of light shining through the darkness.

The Wanderers

The Moon, when it was up, was by far the brightest object in the night sky, dwarfing the pinpricks of the stars and planets. However, the early sky-watchers did become aware that, while most stars retained their patterns and relative positions as they wheeled across the sky, a handful of heavenly bodies followed their own paths. They wandered across the constellations, apparently independent of them. These were the planets – the name means "wanderer" in Greek.

The Wheeling Sky

Because they did not have telescopes, the early sky-watchers were only aware of the five brightest

---

Did You Know?

The Moon takes over 27 days to travel around the Earth. It always keeps the same side facing the Earth.

planets: Mercury, Venus, Mars, Jupiter and Saturn. Among the first astronomers were the ancient Babylonians, who drew star maps to record their observations. They noticed that every 24 hours the patterns of the stars seemed to move in a complete circle from east to west. The hub of that circle seemed to be a star we now know as the North Star, or Polaris. The North Star is so close to the hub that it describes only a very small circle itself. It therefore remains to all intents and purposes fixed in the north. It is a very useful navigational aid, which has been used for centuries.

In this time-lapse photograph, the North Star seems to remain almost motionless, while the other bodies in the sky wheel around it, showing as curving streaks of light.

Sun and Moon Cycles

The Sun and the Moon did not seem to obey the same rules as the starry constellations. They too moved from east to west, but more slowly than the stars. The stars seemed to overtake them. It took about 27½ days for the Moon to be back in the position among the stars where it had started. It appeared to be completely lapped by the wheeling constellations. That 27½ day period is known as a "sidereal month".

The Sun moved even more slowly than the Moon against the stars. The Babylonians calculated its rhythm by watching the times at which some stars seemed to rise in the evening and set in the morning, and their relative positions to the Sun. It took the Sun 365¼ days to be completely lapped by the constellations.

The Babylonians also noticed that the Moon changed shape. It gradually changed from a slender crescent (new moon) to a complete disk (full moon) and then back again to a sliver. From one new moon to the next is 29½ days, which we call the "synodic month."

Foretelling the Future

The Babylonian astronomers discovered from their close studies of the Moon and the Sun that they could accurately foretell when the Moon would pass directly in front of the Sun to cause a solar *eclipse*. They could also predict when the Earth would be directly between the Sun and the Moon, casting a shadow on the Moon to form a lunar eclipse. The power to foresee these events, which the populace considered to be evil omens, made the star-gazers highly respected and somewhat feared.

The Apollo 12 team, on their way to the second lunar landing, saw the unique sight of the Sun disappearing behind the dark disk of the Earth.

The Babylonians also studied the movements of the planets and incorporated them into their theories of *astrology*. They believed they could analyze character and foretell the future of individuals by knowing where the planets were at the time of that person's birth.

Early Astronomers

The first attempts to produce a scientific theory for the way the Solar System worked was made by Greek astronomers. Anaximander (c610-c546 BC) speculated that the Earth was cylindrical and that the heavens rotated around it once every day. Aristarchus of Samos, in the 3rd century BC, was ahead of his time. He believed that everything rotated around the Sun. He also calculated fairly accurately the relative sizes of the Earth and the Moon.

Unfortunately for astronomy, Aristotle (384-322 BC) had such personal authority that his theory – that the Earth was the unmoving center of the Solar System around which everything else rotated – became the standard explanation for the next 1,800 years. Aristotle believed that the Sun, the Moon and the planets were attached to the surfaces of translucent spheres, which performed complex movements around a stationary Earth at the center.

The Awkward Planets

Because Aristotle's theories held sway until the 16th century AD, they created some headaches for astronomers. Some planets seemed to slow down and stop in the course of their westward journeys. They went in the opposite direction, west to east, for a while before resuming their original paths. Mars did this every two years, moving in "retrograde motion" for two months each time, before getting back to normal. Saturn and Jupiter did the same thing, at intervals of 12½ and 13 months respectively.

Between AD 125 and 150, the Alexandrian scholar

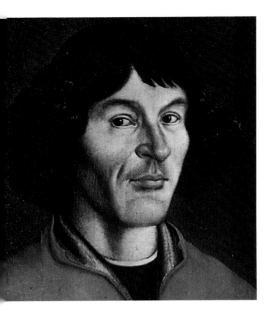

Nicolaus Copernicus overturned the old traditional doctrine that the Earth was the center of the Solar System. His theory that it was more logical for the Sun to be viewed as the center around which all the planets orbit made more sense.

Ptolemy devised a solution to this problem. He proposed that planets rotated in small "epicycles" as they made their way around their major orbits. This theory accounted for the apparent reversal of course every so often. With some astute, but complex, calculations, it kept astronomers reasonably happy for 1,500 years.

Earth Versus Sun

This Earth-centered, or "geocentric," theory of the universe became known as the Ptolemaic system. It was not seriously challenged until the early 1500s. Then a Polish monk, Nicolaus Copernicus, developed his own idea that the Sun was the center of the universe, with the planets orbiting it. This Sun-centered, or "heliocentric," version of the Solar System solved many of the problems thrown up by the Ptolemaic theory. It explained the retrograde motions of Mars, Saturn, and Jupiter. If they were farther away from the Sun than the Earth, Earth's swifter orbit would cause an illusion of retrograde motion as it overtook the orbits of the slower planets.

Mathematicians and New Technology

Early in the 17th century, Johannes Kepler, a German mathematician and astronomer, showed that planetary orbits were elliptical, not the perfect circles of Aristotle and Ptolemy. He also demonstrated that a planet's speed increases as it approaches the Sun and decreases as it gets farther away. In addition, he proved that there is a link between a planet's distance from the Sun and the time it takes to complete one orbit.

At about the same time, the Italian, Galileo Galilei, built himself one of the newly invented telescopes. For the first time, astronomers were able to see details that would revolutionize their understanding of the universe. Galileo discovered craters on the Moon and perceived that Venus had phases, like the Moon, as it orbited the Sun. Looking away from the Sun, Galileo also dis-

Did You Know?
The Moon is a completely silent place. Noise cannot be heard because there is no air to carry sounds from one place to another.

covered the four major moons orbiting Jupiter; they became known as the Galilean moons in his honor.

Galileo was put under house arrest by the Catholic Church for daring to state that the Earth was not the most important body in the universe. However, astronomy was now moving firmly out of the clutches of the priests and into the hands of serious scientists. All over Europe, scientific societies were being formed and observatories built.

Into the Modern Age

In 1687, the great English scientist and mathematician, Sir Isaac Newton, published his "Principia Mathematica," in which he developed his Theory of Gravity. This showed that everything in the universe exerts a gravitational pull, that this increases with the mass of the object, and that gravitational pulls on an object weaken as it moves away from the source of the pull.

Newton's brilliant mathematics ushered in the age of modern astronomy, in which calculations in math and physics can leap ahead to describe objects in the universe before they have been reached by space probes or seen through telescopes.

The Hubble Space Telescope, launched in 1990, has the potential to let us look deeper into space than ever before. In November, 1990, it observed its first faint quasar, billions of light-years from Earth.

Planet Earth

Earth is the third planet from the Sun, orbiting the fiery star at an average distance of 93,000,000 miles (150,000,000 kilometers). At perihelion (when its orbit comes closest to the Sun), the Earth is 91,500,000 miles (147,100,000 kilometers) away. At aphelion (when it is farthest away), the distance is 94,500,000 miles (152,100,000 kilometers).

With a diameter at the *equator* of 7,926 miles (12,756 kilometers), The Earth is the fifth largest — or fifth smallest — of the planets in terms of volume. However, the materials of which it is made give Earth great density. It is the densest of all the planets, with a *"relative density"* 5·5 times that of water. Mighty Jupiter's mass is 318 times that of Earth, yet its density is only 1·3 times that of water. Much of Earth's density is

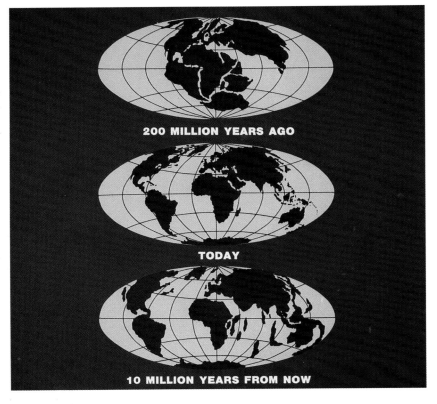

200 MILLION YEARS AGO

TODAY

10 MILLION YEARS FROM NOW

In the course of millions of years, the land masses and seas of Earth have changed position and shape as the tectonic plates forming the planet's crust have slid slowly over the molten magma below.

due to its central core, which is composed of a mixture of heavy nickel and iron, and has a relative density close to 13 times that of water. The Earth is not a perfect sphere. Its circumference round the equator is 24,902 miles (40,075 kilometers). Measured around the poles, it is 24,860 miles (40,008 kilometers). So the planet is somewhat flattened, with a slightly bulging waistline. Its shape is caused by centrifugal force generated by the spinning of the planet on its axis.

In this Apollo 15 picture of the Earth, taken as the astronauts were heading home from the Moon, South America and part of West Africa are visible through the clouds and great swirling weather systems over the southern Atlantic.

The Sun and the Seasons

The Earth's axis, the imaginary line running through the center of the Earth from pole to pole, is not vertical to the plane of the planet's orbit. It tilts at an angle of 23° from the vertical. Because of the tilt, the Sun favors the northern hemisphere for six months of its twelve-month orbit, and the southern hemisphere for the second six months. The temperature cycle of the seasons depends on the tilt. In the northern hemisphere, the axis leans most directly toward the Sun at the summer solstice in June. At the winter solstice in December, the axis in the northern hemisphere leans most directly away from the Sun. The cycle in the southern hemisphere is the direct opposite, so that the southern winter coincides with the northern summer.

Slow Sky Change

Over a very long period, some 26,000 years, the Earth's axis swings around to complete a circular turn. This is caused by the gravitational pulls of the Sun and the Moon on the bulge around the Earth's equator. The movement is so slow that, even over a few centuries, it makes little difference. However, over thousands of years, this *precession* changes the areas of the sky toward which the Earth's axis points. Currently the northern end of the Earth's axis is decorated toward Polaris, the North Star. However, in a few thousand years, it will be pointing in a different direction and Polaris will no longer be the North Star.

When ancient Mediterranean astronomers named the constellations 4,500 years ago, they thought they had covered all the visible star patterns. Other

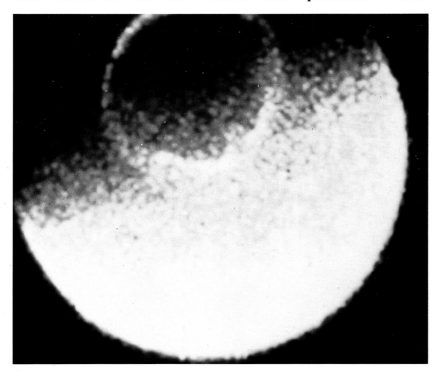

Taken from the Dynamics Explorer spacecraft 14,000 miles (22,000 kilometers) above Earth, this false-color image shows the entire aurora oval over the planet's North Pole.

astronomers, thousands of years later, knew of the old names which had been handed down, but wondered why there was a whole area of starry sky without names. The reason was that the direction of the Earth's axis 4,500 years ago was totally different. A whole area of sky, which had been permanently below the horizon of those early constellation-namers, was now visible.

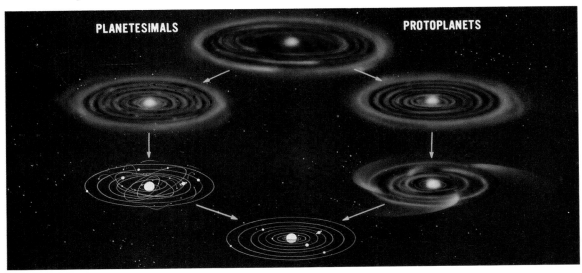

Planetary Workshop

Scientists believe that the Earth came into being, along with the rest of the Solar System, about 4,600,000,000 years ago, as a side effect of the birth of the Sun. Gases and dust formed into lumps of matter orbiting the new star. The force of gravity began to draw the smaller lumps toward the bigger ones, and a process of amalgamation began. After a while, there were swarms of sizable bodies. Some measured up to 620 miles (1,000 kilometers) across. These *planetesimals* all orbited the Sun in the same direction. The process of attraction and collision continued. Finally, there were just a few very large lumps left. They continued to "mop up" the scattered, unattached debris.

Toward the outer edge of the circling cloud of gas, dust and planetesimals, away from the heat of the young Sun, water, ammonia, and methane were frozen into crystal form. They combined with hydrogen and helium, and the outer planets – great gas giants – started to form.

Closer in, where liquids and ice could not survive, the rocky and metallic elements became the far denser bodies of the four "terrestrial planets." Mercury, Venus,

Planetesimals, the building blocks of the planets, range in bulk from specks of grit to sizable satellites hundreds of miles across. The protoplanets mopped them up by accretion, to reach the size and form they are now.

Earth and Mars. They were heated twice: by the radiated energy of the Sun, and also by the internal heat generated by the collapse of the planet under its own of gravity and the impact of attracted space debris on its surface.

Fire and Water

As the infant Earth consolidated, its internal heat became so fierce that it caused the solids to melt. The heavier elements in the planet's make-up were drawn down into the center. Lighter elements, including gases, moved to the surface. This surface began to form a *crust*. Above it, an *atmosphere* began to form from the gases ejected through the cooling crust by the pressures

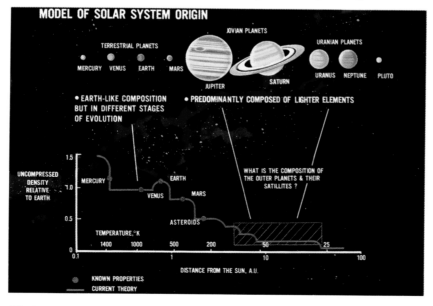

The planets fall into two main groups. The inner, or terrestrial, planets – Mercury, Venus, Earth and Mars – have roughly similar size and solid composition. The outer planets – Jupiter, Saturn, Uranus and Neptune - are many times larger, and of mainly gaseous composition, so they are known as gas giants. Pluto, the outermost planet, is the odd one out, small and similar in make-up to the terrestrial planets.

within. They included carbon dioxide, nitrogen and water vapor. This was a world of active volcanoes in a landscape pockmarked with the impacts of meteorites. The Earth's gravitational pull held onto the atmosphere being created from the volcanic emissions. Volcanic steam condensed to form thick clouds that blanketed the planet. The surface continued to cool. Eventually, the clouds began to pour down rain. It was a rain that lasted for millions of years.

The most ancient rocks found on Earth, other than meteorite fragments, are about 3,800,000,000 years old. They come from this period of Earth's early history, while the rains were playing their part in the long cycles of cooling, cracking, re-melting, and re-cooling in the thickening crust.

The rains created the first oceans. By the time the Earth's surface had cooled enough to interrupt the almost endless cycle of evaporation and condensation, the planet had begun to demonstrate its unique character. It is the only body in the Solar System with a surface covered largely by water.

The First Stirrings

The great cloak of water over the Earth affected the atmosphere. It dissolved some of the gaseous elements in the air, making the atmosphere thinner. Composed

In this composite satellite image of the Earth's biosphere, high concentrations of marine phytoplanktons (tiny sea plants) show up red and orange. On land, dark green indicates rain forests. Lighter green shows other forests, farmland and grassland. Light yellow indicates poor growing areas. Dark yellow areas are even less productive, such as deserts.

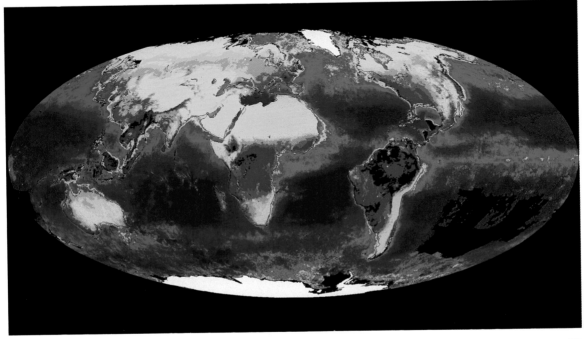

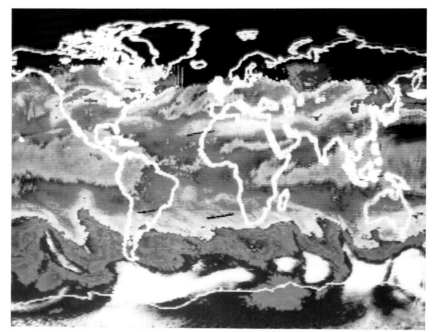

These Nimbus 7 images show ozone concentrations throughout the planet and weather changes over a two-day period. Ozone levels increase from black via violet, red, yellow, green, light blue and dark blue to white. Polar night areas, shown black, were not scanned.

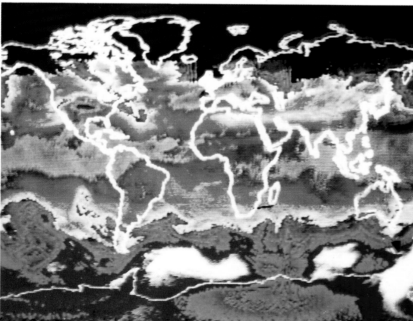

mainly of carbon dioxide and nitrogen, it also included ammonia, carbon monoxide, hydrogen and methane. There was no oxygen yet. Oxygen is essential to nearly all of today's life-forms, but in the beginning, primitive life-forms were necessary to create the oxygen.

Scientists who study the origins of the Earth have conducted many experiments. Gases found in that early atmosphere have been mixed with water and subjected to certain natural traumas such as ultraviolet radiation and the high voltage discharges typical of electrical storms and lightning bolts. Complex substances have been formed as a result. These materials include carbon chemicals and amino acids. Both are fundamental to living matter. The warm, shallow lakes and ocean margins of Earth were ideal cauldrons for this witches' brew, or *"primordial soup,"* as it is sometimes called. It stewed, waiting for the right exposure to ultraviolet rays from the Sun, or lightning strikes from the rumbling clouds. Once the new, biologically active, molecular chains were set in motion, they could sink into the protective depths of their watery environment. There, protected from prolonged exposure to harmful ultraviolet radiation, they could begin to evolve.

Fossil Ancestors
In Swaziland, in southern Africa, scientists have found fossils of primitive, bacterium-like cells in rock which is known to be 3,400,000,000 years old. These cells were capable of splitting and passing on *molecules* of *DNA.* DNA is the code-bearing structure that guarantees that new cells, and more complex bodies, reproduce the characteristics of their parents.

The new cells fed on the "soup" from which they were fashioned. When that began to run out, they adapted to a form that could feed itself through *photosynthesis.* This process needs water, carbon dioxide, the pigment chlorophyll that makes plants green – and sunlight. The new life-form was a tiny blue-green alga. In the presence of sunlight it could turn water and carbon dioxide into sugars and oxygen.

Building an Atmosphere
Blue-green algae were Earth's predominant life-form for hundreds of times longer than humans have existed on Earth. Over hundreds of millions of years,

the algae colonized the planet. These primitive plants pumped out so much oxygen that the atmosphere of the Earth was radically altered. The way was cleared for oxygen-consuming animals to develop. Oxygen-producing plants provided them with food as well as an atmosphere they could breathe.

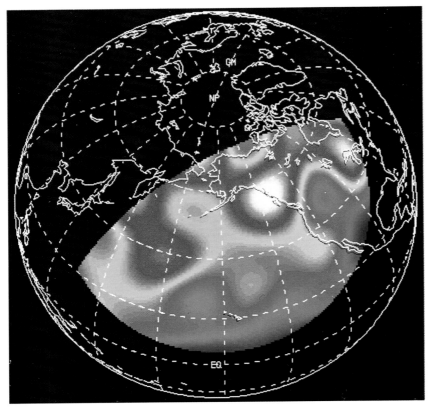

Ozone concentrations in this image increases from blue via green, yellow, red, and purple to white. They were measured by the Dynamics Explorer satellite in 1981. The sharp division from yellow to red shows the pattern of high-altitude jetstream winds.

Oxygen also built a protective barrier of ozone. This is a special form of oxygen that is found only in the upper levels of the atmosphere. It shields living things from the Sun's ultraviolet rays. Life-forms that could leave the protection of the water and exist on dry land were able to develop.

Ceaseless Motion

Today's Earth is still geologically active. Modern volcanic eruptions remind us of the gigantic powers still churning not far beneath our feet. More than 500 volcanoes are still considered active because they have erupted in recorded historic times. About 80 of them are on the floor of the oceans.

Volcanoes usually give some sort of warning that

they are about to erupt. They rumble, and minor lava releases or shape changes occur. Earthquakes, on the other hand, strike without warning though scientists are increasingly able to predict them. Both volcanoes and earthquakes are related to the slow but ceaseless movements of the Earth's structure.

A section cut across a model of the Earth reveals a central core of nickel-iron. Its temperature is 6,690°F (3,700°C), which would melt the center if it was not under such intense pressure. The inner core has a diameter of 1,390 miles (2,400 kilometers). It is surrounded by an outer core of molten iron and nickel, and smaller amounts of silicon. This outer core is 1,400 miles (2,250 kilometers) thick. Around it is the Earth's mantle. This layer of dense rock is 1,800 miles (2,900 kilometers) thick. Some of the rocks remain in a semimolten state. On top of the mantle is the Earth's outer layer, the crust. It varies in thickness from around 3·75 miles (6 kilometers) beneath the oceans to 40 miles (64 kilometers) in mountainous regions on land.

Tectonic Plates

Much of the heat inside the Earth originated in the planet's creation. Yet, new heat is constantly being produced. Some of it stems from the *radioactive decay*

The Himalayas, pictured from directly above by astronauts aboard the space shuttle, reveal their patterns of ridges and valleys outlined in snow and ice.

of minerals in the mantle and the crust. Heat creates convection. In this process, heated molecules rise, travel sideways while cooling, and sink again after cooling. Massive convection currents within the Earth cause slow, unstoppable movements of segments of the upper mantle. These mantle segments, with their topping of oceanic or continental crust, are known as *tectonic plates.*

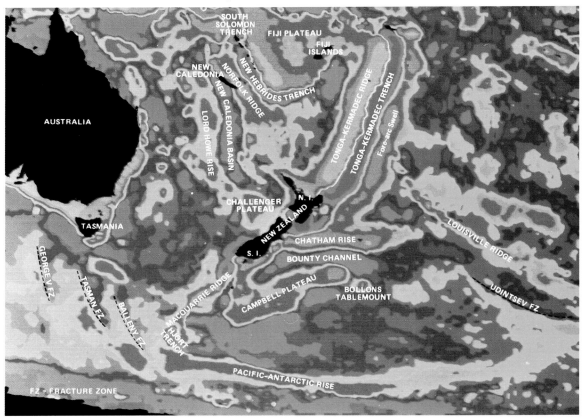

The Jet Propulsion Laboratory's Seasat oceanographic satellite produced this image of the southwest Pacific Ocean. It shows that the ocean bed is as full of mountains and valleys as the land.

The Earth's surface is divided into a number of these "rafts" of rock. They all fit together like the pieces of a vast jigsaw puzzle floating on a semi-molten layer of the mantle called the *asthenosphere.* Sometimes the convection currents pull the plates apart. Sometimes they slide them past one another, or push them into slow head-on collisions. Many of the Earth's mountain ranges were piled up by the slow collision of the plates. Sometimes one plate slides underneath another. Then, the friction can melt already hot rocks into molten magma. It builds up in underground pockets until it forces its way through the crust in volcanic eruptions.

Mexico's Sierra Madre Oriental Mountains form a barrier of curving folds against the desert of the Central Mexican Plateaux.

Slow Slow, Quick Quick, Slow

On the beds of oceans, there are ridges where plates move apart. The gap is constantly replenished with molten rock from below. The motion sometimes sticks along the slip lines. When it jolts onward again, an earthquake may accompany the sudden movement.

In addition to building mountain ranges, tectonic movement can release the molten material that surfaces as volcanic islands. It is also responsible for the slow drift of continents.

The Air Above

The Earth's atmosphere is as unique as its water cover and shifting crust. The air breathed at ground level is 78·08% nitrogen, 20·94% oxygen, 0·93% argon, and varying amounts of water vapor and other gases. In the upper atmosphere, solar ultraviolet radiation changes some of the oxygen into ozone. The ozone absorbs ultraviolet radiation, creating a warm layer. This seals in the weather below it and protects life from unfiltered ultraviolet radiation, which would destroy it.

The air envelope around the Earth also acts as a friction shield. It burns up the billions of meteors that bombard the planet every day, most the size of specks of dust.

At an altitude of about 100 miles (160 kilometers), there is an invisible barrier created by the effect of sunlight on gases in the atmosphere. This reflects some types of radio waves and lets others through. Long-distance radio broadcasts are bounced off the barrier to reach their destinations. Television broadcasts and some types of radio emissions pass through the barrier and need artificial reflectors, such as satellites, to achieve transmissions around the curvature of the planet.

NASA's Nimbus-B satellite used infrared technology to measure temperature, water vapor and ozone in the Earth's atmosphere. It also carried out a number of weather experiments from an orbit 690 miles (1,110 kilometers) high.

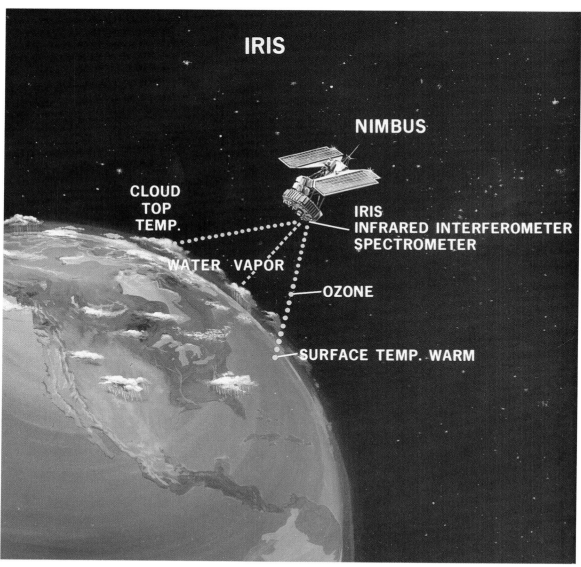

IRIS

NIMBUS

CLOUD TOP TEMP.

IRIS
INFRARED INTERFEROMETER SPECTROMETER

WATER VAPOR

OZONE

SURFACE TEMP. WARM

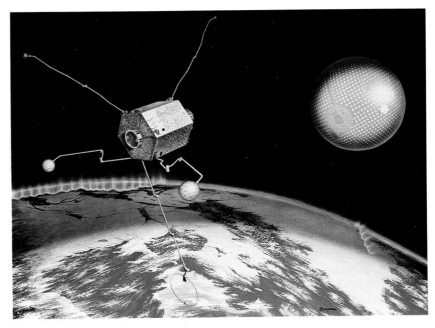

This satellite was designed to measure the upper atmosphere of the Earth during intense solar activity. The NASA vessel split into two separate units after reaching orbit. The six-sided cylinder unit measured radio and radiation emissions while the sphere recorded air density and heat.

Wind and Weather

Earth's weather takes place in the lowest layer of atmosphere, called the troposphere. This is 5 miles (8 kilometers) deep at the poles, and 10 miles (16 kilometers) deep at the equator. Hot, light air rises above the tropics, the wide band of hot climate stretching around the Earth on either side of the equator. Cold polar air moves in to replace it, but is, in turn, heated up and also rises. This constant movement of air is the basis of the planet's wind systems, although the spinning of the Earth also has an effect on wind direction.

The tropics are also the main engine of Earth's rain system. Every year about 368,000 cubic miles (450,000 cubic kilometers) of water rises as vapor from the

This Apollo 9 image shows a huge cyclonic storm system over the Pacific Ocean in March, 1969. Its white clouds contrast starkly with the darkness of space.

oceans, heated by the Sun. The vapor forms clouds and is eventually condensed by cooling. It then falls back to Earth as rain or snow.

Earth has a solid metal core. Around it, deep in the planet, is a layer of molten metal. The spinning of Earth creates swirling currents in this molten metal. In ways not properly understood, this turns Earth into a giant magnet, with invisible lines of magnetic force forming a magnetic field around the planet. These lines move from south to north, and cause compass needles to point in the direction of the North Pole.

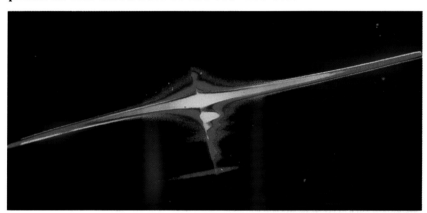

In an ultraviolet photograph of Earth taken from the Moon's surface by an Apollo 16 astronaut in 1972, ultraviolet emissions of hydrogen extend in a bright line to a distance of 40,000 miles (65,000 kilometers) on each side of the planet.

Skylab 3 took this dramatic view of Hurricane Ellen as it rotated counterclockwise over the Atlantic Ocean in September, 1973.

The Moon

The Moon, although smaller than the Earth, is much closer to the Earth in size than any other satellite is to its parent planet in the entire Solar System. For this reason, and because the Moon is so intimately connected with the Earth, the Earth-Moon system is often regarded as a "double planet."

The Moon is 2,160 miles (3,476 kilometers) in diameter. It orbits Earth at an average distance of 238,860 miles (384,400 kilometers). It was formed, like the rest of the Solar System, 4,600 million years ago. Most probably, it followed the same processes of accretion – attracting and mopping up smaller pieces of material – as the Earth and the other terrestrial planets. Its composition is different from that of the Earth. So the theory that it broke away from the Earth early in the life of the Solar System is unlikely. Perhaps it was formed close to Earth.

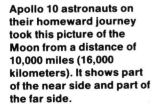

Apollo 10 astronauts on their homeward journey took this picture of the Moon from a distance of 10,000 miles (16,000 kilometers). It shows part of the near side and part of the far side.

Perhaps it formed far away, to be "snared" by Earth's gravitational pull later. However it developed, the Moon is currently moving away from the Earth at the rate of about 1¼ inches (3 centimeters) every year.

Tidal Power

The strong pull between Earth and Moon, together with the pull of the Sun, is responsible for the patterns of tidal behavior on Earth. The rise and fall of tides follow the pull of the Moon on the land as well as the sea. On the side of the Earth closest to the Moon, the sea bulges to produce a high tide. However, the Moon also exerts a pull on the land. In effect, this force pulls the land away from the sea on the far side of the Earth. Water moves to fill the gap, causing tidal bulges on opposite sides of the Earth simultaneously.

When the Sun and the Moon are in line with the Earth, their combined pull creates especially high and low tides. These "spring tides" coincide with the time of full and new moons in the Moon's 29½-day cycle. The friction of tidal waters against their beds is actually slowing the Earth down. The time of Earth's rotation is being reduced by 0·001 seconds per day every century. Four hundred million years ago, the Earth's rotational day was 22 hours long.

The Earth's gravitational effect on the Moon is expressed in the flexing of rock, for there is no liquid on the Moon. This flexing has slowed down the Moon's rotation. It now rotates at exactly the same speed as its orbit, which means that the same face is always seen from Earth.

This view of the far side of the Moon was taken by Apollo 8, the first manned spacecraft to circle the Moon.

The Nearest Neighbor

Even without a telescope, it is easy to make out features on the Moon. Because it is close, it looms large, lit by reflected sunlight. Early Moon-observers, who started to use telescopes in the first decade of the 17th century, referred to the large, dark areas which are visible to the naked eye as "maria," or seas. Galileo described the hundreds of small craters as "spots." Later observations have shown that both "seas" and "spots" are the impact craters of meteorites. The great dark regions are smooth-floored, because volcanic activity has filled them with lava flows.

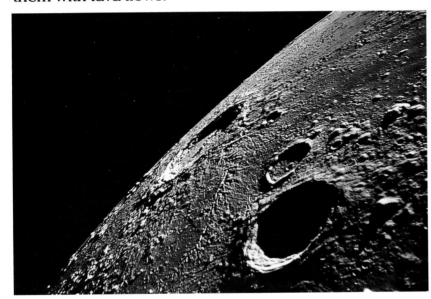

The great crater Copernicus is the one nearest the horizon in this picture taken from the Apollo 12 spacecraft, which landed near a "ray" extending out from the crater. Smaller craters can be seen in the foreground.

Earth, with its atmosphere, water, winds, and active core and mantle, has smoothed away nearly all traces of its early meteorite scarring. The Moon, on the other hand, has no atmosphere, because its weak gravity could not retain one. It is windless and waterless, so it displays the meteorite scars of millions of years sharply defined in its dead surface.

Moon Phases

The Moon we see in our sky, white with reflected sunlight, proceeds dependably every "synodic month" of 29½ days through its phases. Because the new moon is almost in line with the Sun and sets at the same time, we see nothing of it. A few nights later, we see the waxing crescent, which many people call the new moon. The waxing Moon climbs higher as it grows

rounder. It reaches its first quarter after about a week,
sailing high in the sky by sunset, and not setting until
about midnight. When it is at its first quarter, we see half
of its disk illuminated and half in darkness. The imaginary line between dark and light is called the ter-
minator. It is a good place to look at the Moon with a
telescope; the sides of the craters are thrown into high
relief by the shadow. The Moon sets later and later as it
moves east against the stars. About two weeks after the
new moon comes the full moon, rising in the east at
sunset and staying in sight all night. During its waning
period, the Moon does not rise until late at night. At its
last quarter, it rises about midnight, once more showing
exactly half of its face in light – the other half this time.
Finally, it is new – and invisible – again.

About one-third of the
Moon, as seen in this
Apollo 17 picture, is
permanently turned away
from the Earth. Apollo 17
made the final landing in
the Apollo series.

Scouting the Territory

The Russians first showed us the far side of the Moon. In October, 1959, their Luna 3 spacecraft sent pictures of the unknown "back side" of the Moon back to Earth. The previous month, Luna 2 had been the first man-made object to land on the Moon. The far side of the Moon turned out to be less interesting than the familiar side. There are far fewer lava-filled "seas," and the impact craters are closer together than on the near face. There is substantial overlapping of craters. Scientists believe that the far side may have a thicker crust than the near side, making it more difficult for volcanic eruptions to break through.

In August, 1964, the American Ranger 7 spacecraft made a hard landing on the Moon. Transmitting TV images throughout its mission, it gave us the first real close-ups of the Moon's surface. In January, 1966, the Russian Luna 9 soft-lander made a controlled landing and settled many arguments by not immediately sinking into engulfing lunar dust. It sent back detailed pictures of a rock- and crater-strewn lava plain.

By August, 1966, NASA had carried out a high-resolution photo-survey of the whole Moon, using five Orbiter craft working between 30 miles (50 kilometers) and 3,730 miles (6,000 kilometers) above the surface. During the same period, they also put down five Surveyor soft-landers. They scanned the terrain with TV cameras and carried out remote-controlled experiments to identify surface material.

Commander Neil Armstrong was the first human to set foot anywhere in the universe beyond his home planet. He is pictured after returning to the Lunar Module before he rejoined the Command Module to return to Earth.

"One small step . . . " An "alien" foot and footprint in the lunar soil. Undisturbed by winds or any other atmospheric effects, the footprints of Neil Armstrong and the other astronauts could remain unchanged for millions of years.

53

"Buzz" Aldrin, pictured here with a soil-scoop, and Neil Armstrong, collected 50 pounds (22 kilograms) of Moon samples during the Apollo series.

The First Footsteps

On 20 July, 1969, a man first set foot on the Moon. It was an American foot, belonging to Commander Neil Armstrong of the Apollo 11 mission, who uttered the famous words, "That's one small step for man, one giant leap for mankind." Preparations had included a ten-orbit flight around the Moon by Apollo 8 in December, 1968, and a "dress rehearsal" in which Apollo 10's Lunar Excursion Module (LEM) came within 16 kilometers (10 miles) of the Moon's surface during four orbits, in May, 1969.

Neil Armstrong and Edwin "Buzz" Aldrin, pilot of the Apollo 11 LEM, set up measuring equipment on the Moon's surface. They collected 50 pounds (22 kilograms

of rock and soil samples for analysis back on Earth. Because lunar gravity is only one-sixth that of Earth's, the first Moon-walkers felt as if they were moving in slow motion. After 2½ hours on the Moon's surface, Armstrong and Aldrin returned to the LEM. They had a short sleep and then launched the LEM back up into lunar orbit. It docked with the orbiting command module piloted by Michael Collins and returned to Earth.

Lunar Booty

Between July, 1969, and December, 1972, there were six successful Apollo missions. All collected rock and soil samples, and three were equipped with "moon

One of the lunar surface samples collected on the Apollo 12 mission. It is a fine-grained igneous rock with needles of the mineral feldspar.

The various Moon buggies, or Lunar Roving Vehicles (LRVs), used by the Apollo astronauts to move around on the lunar terrain caught the imagination of the general public. This one was used by the Apollo 16 team.

No Earth plant could grow in the airless conditions of the Moon, but these ferns are thriving in the nutrients present in Moon soil. This experiment with Apollo 11 material, was carried out at Mission Control, Houston. The flourishing, dark-colored ferns are in direct contact with Moon soil, while the lighter, less vigorous ferns are growing in a synthetic medium.

buggies.'' These lunar roving vehicles (LRV) allowed the astronauts to go farther afield and carry more samples. The total of Moon samples brought back by the Apollo missions was 850 pounds (386 kilograms).

Between 1970 and 1976, the Russians perfected techniques of remote-controlled sample collection. "Driven" by radio transmissions from Earth, the Russian "Lunokhod" vehicles, powered by solar panels, took

Did You Know?

Unlike Earth, which has been continuously worn away, the surface of the Moon has not been attacked by wind and water. Rocks brought back to Earth by astronauts have probably been lying in the same position for 3,000,000,000 years without moving a fraction of an inch.

photographs and drilled out core samples. The last Moon probe in the series was Luna 24, which landed back in the Soviet Union on August 22, 1976.

The Moon explorers walked on a world which seemed geologically "dead," without volcanic activity. Orbiting spacecraft did detect some radioactive areas, and in one region, the gas radon was being vented to the surface. Temperatures on the dust- and rock-covered surface varied from $-280°F$ $(-140°C)$ below zero at night, to $230°F$ $(110°C)$ in the daytime. The rocks collected for analysis contain high proportions of the elements aluminum and titanium. Some contain

"Buzz" Aldrin is seen here standing in front of the Lunar Excursion Module (LEM) "Eagle" – the astronauts' home for the 21½ hours of their stay on the Moon's surface.

MOON FACTS

Least distance from Earth: 224,300 miles
(361,000 kilometers)
Average distance from Earth: 238,860 miles
(384,400 kilometers)
Greatest distance from Earth: 250,400 miles
(403,000 kilometers)
Temperature on sunlit side: 230°F (110°C)
Temperature on dark side: −280°F (−140°C)
Diameter across equator: 2,160 miles
(3,476 kilometers)
Atmosphere: None
Length of day: 27·3 Earth days
Length of year: 1 Earth year
Length of lunar month: 29½ Earth days

Opposite: Planet Earth sets over the lunar horizon in this sequence of pictures taken by Apollo 10 astronauts from their module above the Moon's surface.

a compound known as KREEP, high in potassium (chemical symbol K), rare earth elements (REE), and phosphorus (P).

Below: Photomicrographs of lunar sample sections reveal their crystalline structure. This sample, brought back by Apollo 12, is like fine-grained basalt.

Earth, Moon, and Life

Perhaps planet Earth should be called planet Earth-Moon. Certainly, the intimate relationship between Earth and Moon is one of the things that makes Earth unique. It influences water movements, rotation speeds, and certain life cycles and processes. The Moon's influence may also be responsible for some earthquake activity, and the continuing heat of Earth's core may owe something to an earlier time when Earth and Moon were much closer and spun together faster. Some scientists even believe that the life that sets Earth apart in the Solar System would not have been possible without the Earth-Moon interaction. If future space explorers seek out non-terrestrial life among the stars, they may have to concentrate their search on double planets.

In this Seasat image of the Earth's oceans, taken in 1978, we can see the ridges and trenches, mountains, and fracture zones of the ocean bed.

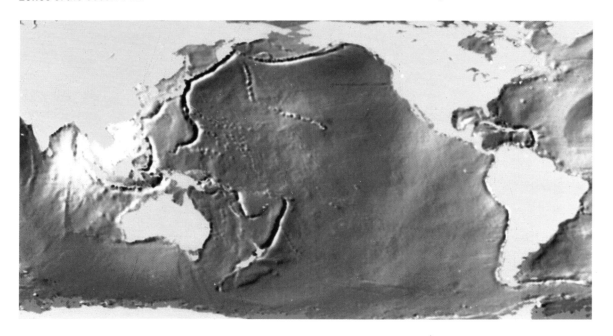

60

Books to Read

INTRODUCTORY READING

Earth: Our Home Base by Isaac Asimov (Gareth Stevens Inc., 1988)

Earth: Our Planet in Space by Seymour Simon (Macmillan, 1984)

Earth: The Ever-Changing Planet by Donald M. Silver (Random House, 1989)

How Did We Find Out the Earth Is Round by Isaac Asimov (Walker & Co., 1972)

Mysteries of the Planet Earth by Franklin M. .Branley (Loadestar Books, 1989)

Our Planet the Earth by Keith Lye (Lerner Publications, 1986)

Our Wonderful Solar System by Richard Adams (Troll Associates, 1983)

Planet Earth by Martyn Bramwell (Franklin Watts, 1987)

Planet Earth by Ruth Radlauer & Charles Stembridge (Children's Press, 1984)

The Planets: Exploring the Solar System by Roy A. Gallant (Macmillan, 1985)

The Planets In Our Solar System by Roy M. Branley (Harper & Row Junior Books, 1987)

Solar System by K. Frazier (Time-Life, 1985)

The Solar System by David Lambert (Franklin Watts, 1984)

The Sun and Its Family by Irving Adler (Harper & Row Junior Books, 1969)

FURTHER READING

Beyond Spaceship Earth: Environmental Ethics and the Solar System edited by Eugene C. Hargrove (Sierra Club Books, 1987)

Biography of a Planet: Geology, Astronomy and the Evolution of Life on Earth by Chet Raymo (Prentice Hall, 1984)

Earth by David Bennett (Bantam Books, 1988)

The Earth by Harold Jefferys (Cambridge University Press, 1976)

The Home Plenet edited by Kevin W. Kelley (Addison-Wesley, 1988)

A Magnet Called Earth by Roy T. Maloney (Dropzone Press, 1989)

New Worlds: In Search of the Planets by Heather Couper & Nigel Henbest (Addison-Wesley, 1986)

Planetary Landscapes by Ronald Greeley (Unwin Hyman, 1987)

Portraits of Earth by Freeman Patterson (Sierra Club Books, 1982)

The Solar System by Susan D. Echaore (Janus Books, 1982)

The Solar System by B. W. Jonnes & Milton Keynes (Pergamon Press, 1984)

A Spaceship Called Earth: Our Living Environment by Mark W. & Margaret E. Parratt (Kendall-Hunter, 1985)

The Story of the Earth by Peter Cattermole & Patrick Moore (Cambridge University Press, 1985)

The Third Planet by Time-Life Books Editors (Time-Life, 1989)

Glossary

ABSOLUTE ZERO The lowest possible temperature in theory: 0 Kelvin, or −459·6° Fahrenheit (−273·15° Celsius).

ALGAE Primitive water-dwelling plants with simple structures.

APHELION An orbiting body's farthest point from the Sun.

ASTEROID One of the thousands of minor planets in the Solar System, mostly under 60 miles (100 kilometers) in diameter.

ASTHENOSPHERE The hot, mobile region of the Earth's mantle, beneath the tectonic plates.

ASTROLOGY The forerunner of astronomy, in which predictions were made about events and human personalities by refering to the position of the Sun, Moon and planets, particularly at the time of a person's birth.

ASTRONOMICAL UNIT (AU) A unit of measurement equal to the Earth's distance from the Sun, about 93,000,000 miles (150,000,000 kilometers).

ATMOSPHERE The envelope of gases around some heavenly bodies, including the Earth.

ATOM The smallest stable component of a chemical element.

CELSIUS SCALE A temperature scale with freezing point at 0° and boiling point at 100°.

COMET A body that orbits the Sun, usually with a very eccentric orbit. When a comet is visible from Earth it trails a tail of gas and dust.

CONSTELLATION One of the 88 named regions that make up the night sky and its stars as seen from Earth.

CRUST The Earth's surface layer, about 20 miles (32 kilometers) thick in continental regions, and some 6 miles (10 kilometers) thick beneath the oceans.

DOPPLER EFFECT The apparent change in a sound or color as it approaches or recedes from Earth.

DNA Deoxyribonucleic acid, a component of living cells that contains heredity information.

ECLIPSE The total or partial blotting out of the light from a body in space by the shadow of another body. When the body of the Moon blots out the Sun, we also call that an eclipse, though the correct term is "occultation."

EQUATOR The surface circle that divides a planet into equal northern and southern hemispheres.

GALAXY A vast system of stars, planets, satellites, gas, and dust held together by the interaction of gravity.

GRAVITY The force of attraction that material bodies in space exert on one another.

INTERSTELLAR SPACE The region of near-vacuum existing between the stars of our galaxy.

LIGHT-YEAR The distance traveled by a ray of light in one year in a vacuum: 63,240 Astronomical Units (AU).

MANTLE The thick layer of rock lying between the Earth's molten core and the surface.

MASS The total quantity of material in a body.

MOLECULE A combination of two or more atoms bound together.

ORBIT The path of a body in space as it moves around another, within the influence of its gravitational field.

PARSEC A unit of distance, usually extending beyond the Solar System: 3·26 light years.

PERIHELION An orbiting body's closest point to the Sun.

PHOTOSYNTHESIS The formation of carbon compounds by green plants from carbon dioxide using the energy of sunlight.

PLANET A body that orbits a star and shines only by reflected light from the star.

PLANETESIMAL Intermediate objects between grains of matter and the planets; the building blocks of the planets.

PRECESSION The slow movement of the Earth's axis, which describes a circle every 26,000 years due to the gravitational pulls of the Sun and the Moon.

PRIMORDIAL SOUP The warm, shallow waters, laced with carbon compounds, in which life may have originated on Earth.

RADIAL VELOCITY The speed at which a body in space approaches or recedes from Earth.

RADIOACTIVE DECAY The disintegration of certain atomic nuclei, with the emission of sub-atomic particles and gamma rays.

RED SHIFT The apparent reddening of the light emitted by another galaxy, showing it is receding.

RELATIVE DENSITY The density of a body relative to the density of water.

SATELLITE A body that orbits a planet.

SOLAR SYSTEM The Sun and all bodies orbiting it.

STAR A self-illuminating body of gas in space.

SUPERNOVA A late stage in the life of some stars, when they explode with a huge release of energy.

TECTONIC PLATE A section of a celestial body's crust moved by geological forces.

Index